PREHISTORIC!

DINOSAURS
OF THE TRIASSIC

by
David West

A+

Smart Apple Media

Published by Smart Apple Media, an imprint of Black Rabbit Books
P.O. Box 3263, Mankato, Minnesota 56002
www.blackrabbitbooks.com

Produced by David West 🧍🧍 Children's Books
6 Princeton Court, 55 Felsham Road, London SW15 1AZ

Designed and illustrated by David West

Special thanks to Dr. Ron Blakey for the maps on page 4 & 5

Library of Congress Cataloging-in-Publication Data

West, David, 1956- author.
Dinosaurs of the Triassic / David West.
    pages cm. -- (Prehistoric!)
Audience: Grade 4 to 6.
Includes index.
ISBN 978-1-62588-083-3 (library binding)
ISBN 978-1-62588-110-6 (paperback)
1. Paleontology--Triassic--Juvenile literature. 2. Dinosaurs--Juvenile literature. I. Title.
QE732.W47 2015
560.1762--dc23
                                2013036557

                        Printed in China
        CPSIA compliance information: DWCB14CP
                            010114

                    9 8 7 6 5 4 3 2 1

Contents

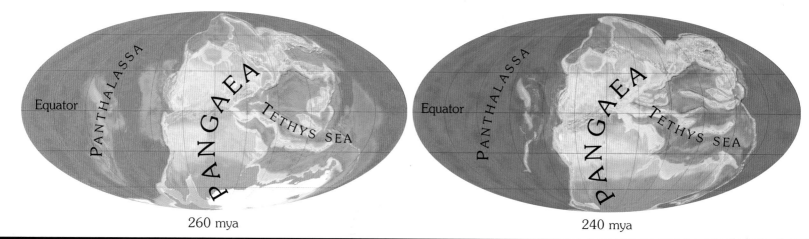

260 mya

240 mya

250 Millions of years ago (mya)

EARLY TRIASSIC

247

240

MIDDLE TRIASSIC

230

235

249 mya Sea surface temperatures of 104°F (40°C) in the tropics.

248 mya Permian Mass Extinction causes 96% of all species to die out.

230 mya The evolution of dinosaurs and the first mammals started.

The Triassic Period

During the Triassic period, Earth's landmass was all one continent, called Pangaea, which means "all the land." To the east, a large gulf, called the Tethys Sea, entered Pangaea. The rest of the ocean is called the Panthalassa, which means "all the sea." By the mid-Triassic, the Pangaea began to separate gradually into two landmasses—Laurasia in the north and Gondwana to the south. The climate was mostly hot and dry with deserts covering the interior. The period ended with another major mass extinction that destroyed many animal groups and allowed dinosaurs to rule the land.

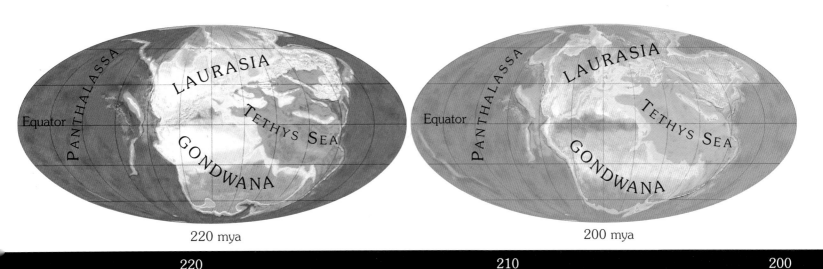

220 mya

200 mya

LATE TRIASSIC

Many of the first dinosaurs evolved during the Late Triassic, including *Plateosaurus*, *Coelophysis*, and *Eoraptor*.

205 mya Triassic-Jurassic Mass Extinction causes about half of all animal species to die out.

LIFE DURING THE TRIASSIC

The Triassic began after the Permian–Triassic extinction event. It took well into the middle of the period for life to recover fully. **Therapsids** and **archosaurs** were the main land animals during this time. A specialized subgroup of archosaurs, the dinosaurs, first appeared in the Late Triassic. The first true mammals, which were a subgroup of the therapsids, also evolved during this period as did the first flying reptiles, the **pterosaurs**.

The oceans were home to air-breathing reptiles that had similar lifestyles to modern dolphins and seals.

Ticinosuchus

Ticinosuchus was not a dinosaur. It was a member of the family of predatory archosaurs known as **rauisuchians**. Its name means "Ticino River crocodile" after the place in Italy where its **fossils** were found.

Ticinosuchus was quite small for a rauisuchian. But nevertheless, it was a ferocious **predator** that hunted smaller reptiles. *Ticinosuchus's* entire body, even the belly, was covered in thick, armored **scutes** similar to modern crocodiles, but the way it moved was very different.

In this scene from the shores of Triassic Europe, a group of juvenile *Nothosauruses* (2) scatter into the surf to flee from a hungry *Ticinosuchus* (1).

From the structure of its leg bones, **paleontologists** know that the back legs were directly beneath its body rather than out to the side as in modern crocodiles. This suggests that *Ticinosuchus* was a fast runner. Its diet included shellfish and fish. Probably an opportunist, it snacked on carrion and hatchlings.

Ticinosuchus grew to 10 feet (3 m) long and weighed about 100 pounds (45.3 kg).

Arizonasaurus

Like *Ticinosuchus*, *Arizonasaurus* was an archosaur that lived in North America during the early Triassic. Its name means "Arizona Lizard" and is named for the state where its fossils were discovered. It was one of the largest, meat-eating hunters of its time.

Arizonasaurus was the dominant predator, hunting smaller animals and feeding on carrion. It had a large sail on its back, which may have been used as a temperature-regulation device.

An *Arizonasaurus* (1) seizes the opportunity for a quick meal and launches an attack on an *Eocyclotosaurus* (2) that has just surfaced with a freshwater *Coelacanth* (3) in its mouth.

The sail also may have been used in courtship displays. Sharing the environment with *Arizonasaurus* were freshwater **hybodont** sharks, coelacanths, **lungfish**, and **temnospondyl amphibians** such as *Eocyclotosaurus*, rauisuchians such as *Chirotherium*, and various **rhynchosaurs** and **dicynodonts**.

Arizonasaurus was around 20 feet (6.1 m) in length and weighed up to 500 pounds (227 kg).

Herrerasaurus

Herrerasaurus was one of the earliest dinosaurs. It means "Herrera's lizard" and is named after the rancher who discovered it in northwestern Argentina. It has been classified an early **theropod**.

Herrerasaurus moved on its back legs, making it a biped. It had strong hind limbs with short thighs, suggesting it was a swift runner. The tail was partially stiffened, which helped balance the body as it ran. *Herrerasaurus* lived during a time when dinosaurs were small and other

A pair of juvenile *Herrerasauruses* (1), one of which has caught a small lizard, have surprised a group of *Pisanosauruses* (2) in what is today Argentina. In the background, two dicynodonts, called *Ischigualastia*, (3) browse on ferns.

reptiles were more numerous. Smaller dinosaurs, such as *Pisanosaurus* and *Eoraptor,* shared the habitat along with dicynodonts, such as *Ischigualastia,* and **cynodonts** and **aetosaurs**. The climate was warm and moist. The landscape was covered in ferns with **horsetails** and giant conifers growing along the banks of rivers.

Herrerasaurus grew to about 10 feet (3 m) long and weighed 500 pounds (227 kg).

2

Shonisaurus

Shonisaurus means "Lizard from the Shoshone Mountains" after the place where its fossils were found. It was one of the largest **ichthyosaurs** ever to have lived. The largest was *Shastasaurus,* which measured up to 69 feet (21 m).

Shonisaurus looked like a strange fish, but it was an air-breathing aquatic reptile. It had a long, toothless snout, although juveniles had teeth along the end of the snout. Its body was quite deep compared

A pair of *Shonisauruses* (1) head past a coral reef into deep water where they can hunt for squid and other cephalopods. In the background three *Cymbospondyluses* (2) play among schools of fish in this scene from the edge of the Tethys Sea.

with other ichthyosaurs and had long, narrow flippers. It spent much of its time in the deep oceans feeding on squid and other **cephalopods**. Ichthyosaurs, such as *Cymbospondylus*, shared the oceans. They ventured into shallower water to breed and gave birth to live young.

Shonisaurus grew to about 49 feet (15 m) long and weighed about 30 tons (27.2 mt).

Unaysaurus

This sauropod dinosaur is one of the oldest dinosaurs known. *Unaysaurus*, meaning "black water lizard," is closely related to a dinosaur found in Germany. This may indicate that it was quite easy for species to spread across the giant landmass of the time—the supercontinent of Pangaea.

Unaysaurus was a slender, plant-eating dinosaur that walked on its two back legs. It was closely related to *Plateosaurus* (see pages 28–29),

14

In this scene from the middle to late Triassic of what is Brazil today, a pair of *Unaysauruses* (1) run for their lives as a pack of hungry *Pampadromaeuses* (2) attempt to take one down.

which lived slightly later in Europe. It may have competed with other early dinosaurs such as the **sauropod**, *Pampadromaeus*. It had a very theropod-like body with long hind legs and a narrow snout. The two types of teeth found in its jaws, leaf-shaped ones in front and curved ones at the back, show that *Pampadromaeus* probably ate both plants and animals, making it an omnivore.

Unaysaurus grew up to 8 feet (2.4 m) long and weighed 200 pounds (90.7 kg).

Postosuchus

Postosuchus was the top predator during the late Triassic in what is now the southern United States. Its name means "crocodile from Post." Most of its fossils have been found in Post Quarry in Texas. It, and the *Ticinosaurus* and *Arizonasaurus*, were all archosaurs.

Postosuchus had shorter front legs. Scientists think it probably walked some of the time on two legs. It appeared similar to modern crocodiles but, with the legs under the body, it would have been a faster and

16

A *Postosuchus* (1) launches an attack on an unsuspecting *Koskinonodon* (2) from its hiding place. In the background *Placerias* (3) warily approach the lake's edge to drink the water.

more efficient runner. It preyed on the prehistoric crocodiles, amphibians such as the 10-foot-long (3 m) *Koskinonodon*, and dicynodonts such as *Placerias*. These large **herbivores** were up to 11 feet (3.4 m) long and spent much of their time in or close to water. They had sharp beaks to crop vegetation and two small tusks that could be used in self-defense.

Postosuchus grew to 13 feet (4 m) long and weighed 660 pounds (299 kg).

1

Desmatosuchus

Living alongside the early dinosaurs of the Triassic was the aetosaur *Desmatosuchus*. Its name means "Link crocodile." Despite its ferocious appearance, it was a plant eater.

Desmatosuchus had an armored body and a head with a pig-like snout. It used its shovel-like snout to uproot soft plants. Similar to other Aetosaurs, it had heavy, armored plates along its back, tail, and parts of its underside. It differs from them, however, with two rows of

18

A *Desmatosuchus* (1) drinks from a lake as a small *Rutiodon* (2) breaks the surface with a *Xenacanthus* (3) in its mouth. A pair of *Malerisauruses* (4) run away from the disturbance in this scene from the North American Triassic.

spikes along the sides of its back. The largest spikes, above the shoulders, were 18 inches (45 cm) long. These gave it extra protection against predators such as the large crocodile-like *Rutiodon*, which could grow to 25 feet (7.6 m) in length. This predator fed on fish, but it also would have ambushed animals drinking at the edge of a lake or river.

Desmatosuchus was about 15 feet (4.6 m) long and weighed about 500 pounds (227 kg).

2

Euskelosaurus

Euskelosaurus, meaning "true-limbed lizard," was a **prosauropod** living in the woodlands of South Africa during the late Triassic. It was the first dinosaur to be discovered in South Africa. Many individual fossils of this dinosaur have now been found.

Euskelosaurus was one of the largest prosauropods. It was a plant eater that walked on all fours and may have been an ancestor to *Plateosaurus* (see pages 28–29). It was a close relative of two other

Two juvenile *Euskelosauruses* (1) search for vegetation to eat among the tall conifers of a South African woodland. In the background, a group of *Melanorosauruses* (2) migrate to new feeding grounds.

large prosauropods, *Riojasaurus* in South America and the plant eater *Melanorosaurus,* which lived in South Africa at the same time. This giant herbivore had a large body and sturdy limbs, so it probably walked on all four legs. Its leg bones were massive as were later sauropod limb bones, but the feet still maintained the protruding toes.

Euskelosaurus grew to 33 feet (10 m) long and weighed around 2 tons (1.8 mt).

21

1

2

Nothosaurus

During the middle to late Triassic period, a marine reptile called *Nothosaurus* swam in the seas. Its name means, "false reptile." Its fossils have been found in Africa, Europe, and China.

Although *Nothosaurus* spent most of its time at sea, it had to venture onto land to lay its eggs, as modern marine turtles do. Its lifestyle, though, was probably very similar to modern-day seals. It fed on fish by using its long, sharp teeth to capture them. It used its tail and

A pair of female *Nothosauruses* (1) emerge from the sea to lay their legs on land. On the beach, small *Saltopuses* (2) chase dragonflies as *Thecodontosauruses* (3) feed on **cycads** in this scene from Triassic Europe.

webbed feet to swim and steer through the water. Once on shore, it was less athletic and, along with its hatchlings, was at the mercy of predators such as *Ticinosuchus* (see pages 6–7). Other creatures that shared this environment included sauropod dinosaurs such as *Thecodontosaurus* and small **carnivores** called *Saltopus*, which were the size of a cat.

Nothosaurus grew up to 10 feet (3 m) long and weighed 200 pounds (90.7 kg).

1

Coelophysis

Coelophysis was a light and nimble theropod dinosaur. Its name means "hollow form," which refers to its hollow bones. It could run fast on its two back legs, chasing small lizards and insects.

Coelophysis is one of the earliest dinosaurs to be discovered. It had arms and hands adapted for grasping its prey. Its neck and tail were long and slender. It had a long, narrow head with large, forward-facing eyes, which gave it good vision for hunting. Its long snout was crowded

24

Three *Coelophysises* (1) chase after dragonflies through a floodplain in what is now the southwestern United States. In the background, a *Hesperosuchus* (2) chases after a group of *Dromomerons* (3).

with small, sharp, jagged teeth that had fine serrations on both front and back. It probably fed on small fish, lizards, insects, and small **dinosauromorphs** such as *Dromomeron*. It lived alongside other dinosaurs such as *Chindesaurus* and *Daemonosaurus*, and **crocodylomorphs** such as *Hesperosuchus*.

Coelophysis reached a length of 9.8 feet (3 m) and weighed about 33 pounds (15 kg).

Tanystropheus

Tanystropheus was not a dinosaur but a semi-aquatic reptile living during the Triassic period. Its name means "long vertebra," which refers to its long neck with ten very long vertebrae.

Tanystropheus was a fish eater. Its narrow snout, crammed with sharp interlocking teeth, was ideal for catching its slippery prey. Scientists think it perched on rocks and used its long neck to reach fish swimming close to the shore. It may also have walked or swum close

A *Tanystropheus* (1) makes its way down to a rocky shore on the Tethys Sea in this scene from the late Triassic. The pterosaurs, *Peteinosauruses* (2) and the *Eudimorphodons* (3), fly above.

to the bottom of coastal seas and grabbed unsuspecting fish. One of the earliest pterosaurs, the *Eudimorphodon*, competed for fish. These small winged reptiles had long tails with a diamond-shaped flap at the end. Beak-like mouths held 110 sharp teeth that were ideal for snatching fish close to the surface. *Peteinosaurus*, another early pterosaur from this period, fed on insects.

Tanystropheus grew to 20 feet (6.1 m) long and weighed around 300 pounds (136 kg).

27

3

2

Plateosaurus

Plateosaurus, meaning "broad lizard," is a dinosaur that lived about 214 to 204 million years ago in what is now Central and Northern Europe.

Plateosaurus belonged to the group of dinosaurs called prosauropods. It was a relative, but not an ancestor, of the gigantic, long-necked sauropods of the Jurassic and Cretaceous periods. It walked on two legs but may have balanced on its hands when browsing on low vegetation. It fed solely on vegetation and had sharp, but plump, plant-crushing teeth. It used its muscular arms and grasping hands with large claws on

A group of *Plateosauruses* (1) feed on cycads on the edge of an arid region in what is Germany today. Three *Procompsognathuses* (2) run from a lone *Liliensternus* (3) on the hunt for prey. They head for the relative safety of the cycads.

three fingers for defense and feeding. *Plateosaurus* may have been preyed upon by the large, carnivorous *Liliensternus*. This predator used its slashing teeth to disable large prosauropods and its speed to catch smaller prey, such as the 3.3 feet (1 m) long *Procompsognathuses*.

Plateosaurus grew to 26 feet (7.9 m) long and weighed up to 4 tons (3.6 mt).

Animal Listing
Other animals that appear in the scenes.

Cymbospondylus
(pp. 12–13)
ichthyosaur
33 feet (10 m) long
Oceans

Dromomeron
(pp. 24–25)
dinosauromorph
3.3 feet (1 m) long
North America

Eocyclotosaurus
(pp. 8–9)
temnospondyl
3.3 feet (1 m) long
North America, Europe,
Asia, and Australia

Eudimorphodon
(pp. 26–27)
pterosaur
3.3 feet (1 m) wingspan
Europe

Hesperosuchus
(pp. 24–25)
crocodylomorph
3.3 feet (1 m) long
North America

Ischigualastia
(pp. 10–11)
dicynodont
11.5 feet (3.5 m) long
South America

Koskinonodon
(pp. 16–17)
temnospondyl
3 feet (10 m) long
North America

Liliensternus
(pp. 28–29)
theropod dinosaur
16.9 feet (5.1 m) long
Europe

Malerisaurus
(pp. 18–19)
archosaur
3.9 feet (1.2 m) long
India, North America

Melanorosaurus
(pp. 20–21)
sauropodomorph dinosaur
40 feet (12.2 m) long
Africa

Pampadromaeus
(pp. 14–15)
sauropodomorph dinosaur
5 feet (1.5 m) long
South America

Peteinosaurus
(pp. 26–27)
pterosaur
2 feet (60 cm) wingspan
Europe

Pisanosaurus
(pp. 10–11)
ornithischian dinosaur
3.3 feet (1 m) long
South America

Placerias
(pp. 16–17)
dicynodont
11 feet (3.5 m) long
North America

Procompsognathus
(pp. 28–29)
theropod dinosaur
3.3 feet (1 m) long
Europe

Rutiodon
(pp. 18–19)
phytosaur
25 feet (7.6 m) long
North America

Saltopus
(pp. 22–23)
dinosauromorph
3.3 feet (1 m) long
Europe

Thecodontosaurus
(pp. 22–23)
sauropodomorph dinosaur
6.5 feet (2 m) long
Europe

Xenacanthus
(pp. 18–19)
prehistoric shark
2 feet (60 cm) long
Worldwide

Glossary

aetosaur An extinct type of heavily armored, herbivorous archosaur.

archosaur Member of a large group of animals that include crocodiles, birds, dinosaurs, and pterosaurs.

carnivore An animal that eats meat.

cephalopod A marine animal with a set of arms or tentacles which includes octopuses, squid, and extinct ammonites.

crocodylomorphs Members of an important group of reptiles that includes the crocodiles.

cycad A plant with a stout, woody trunk with a crown of large, fern-like, evergreen leaves.

cynodont An extinct mammal-like reptile.

dicynodonts An extinct group of mammal-like reptiles with two tusks.

dinosauromorph A dinosaur-like reptile that possesses some, but not all, of the features of dinosaurs.

fossils The remains of living things that have turned to rock.

herbivore Plant-eating animal.

horsetail A plant often growing in marshy environments.

hybodont A type of extinct genus of shark with two types of teeth and a sharp spike on the dorsal fin.

ichthyosaur A giant marine reptile that resembled a dolphin.

lungfish A freshwater fish that is able to breathe air with the use of its lungs.

ornithischian A type of dinosaur that had a pelvis that was bird-hipped.

paleontologists Scientists who study the forms of life that existed in earlier geologic periods by looking at fossils.

predator An animal that hunts other animals for food.

prosauropod An early herbivorous dinosaur with a long neck and small head that mainly walked on two legs.

pterosaur A flying reptile.

phytosaur An extinct, long-snouted and heavily armored reptile, that looked similar to a modern crocodilian.

rauisuchian A crocodile-like animal with legs beneath the body, rather than spreading outward.

rhynchosaur Extinct, herbivorous reptile with a beak.

sauropod A type of herbivorous dinosaur that had a long neck, a long tail, and walked on four legs.

sauropodomorph A type of long-necked, herbivorous, dinosaur that includes the sauropods and their relatives

scutes Bony, external plates or scales.

temnospondyl amphibian A form of large, extinct, primitive amphibian.

therapsid An extinct group of animals that includes the ancestors of mammals.

theropod A type of dinosaur that moved on two legs. Most of them were carnivorous.

Index